KING ORRY
from Saint to Sovereign

Miles Cowsill   John Hendy

ISBN 0 951350676

25 Corner Farm Road, Staplehurst, Kent, TN12 OPJ

(Photo: John Hendy)

INTRODUCTION

Few passengers who sail to Douglas on board the Isle of Man Steam Packet's luxury flagship, the *King Orry*, will have any idea of her pedigree, of how she was almost the ship that never was or of how she served on the cross Channel link between her home port of Dunkerque and Dover for thirteen years. During the happy days prior to the Channel Tunnel, she carried the blue Wagon-Lits coaches of the only through passenger train to operate between Britain and the European mainland – the fabled Night Ferry.

In those days she was the *Saint Eloi*, proudly carrying the name of the patron saint of her home port, Dunkerque. The city in northern France was, of course, the scene of Operation Dynamo when during nine momentous days in May and June 1940, the remnants of the British Expeditionary Force were snatched from the battered city and its nearby beaches from beneath the guns of the encircling German Army. The Isle of Man Steam Packet Company was there in the thick of it all. It is claimed that its ships rescued more men than those of any other short sea fleet but in its hours of triumph it was to pay dearly, losing the six year old *Mona's Queen*, the three year old *Fenella* and also the veteran steamer, the third *King Orry*.

Fifty years later, a new *King Orry* was ready to grace the Irish Sea. As the fifth ship to carry this illustrious name, she reminds us of the long sea-going traditions which have maintained the vital lifeline from the Isle of Man to the British mainland. She also reminds us, through her French connection, of the Steam Packet's magnificent war effort and of the supreme sacrifice made during the inferno of Dunkerque in those balmy, far-off, days of 1940.

Miles Cowsill   John Hendy
Kilgetty, Pembrokeshire   *May 1992*   Staplehurst, Kent

The ship's bell tells her story – Saint on one side, Sovereign on the other. (John Hendy)

FOREWORD

be very harsh, in order to maintain the vital regular service which the Island community depends on as its 'lifeline'.

Over the years, we have had many ships specially built for the Company, but it often makes more sense to purchase second hand vessels at a much lower cost. In the late 1980's we were seeking a replacement multi-purpose vessel to enable us to improve our year-round passenger service, and eventually secured the ship which this book is about. On a personal note, I have to say that John Hendy told us what a good ship she was at the time we were searching, and his opinion, supported by our own detailed appraisal, has proved to be fully justified.

I hope that you enjoy reading this book as much as I have done, and that you will enjoy sailing across the Irish Sea on the *King Orry* for many years to come.

David Dixon
Managing Director of the
Isle of Man Steam Packet Company.

The Steam Packet Company has always taken great care to acquire ships which will meet its own rather special requirements. They have to be small enough to call at a number of ports around the Irish Sea which are restricted in the length or draft of vessel they can accommodate. At the same time they must be able to operate safely in weather conditions which at times can

First season. The Saint Eloi *leaves Dover for Dunkerque. (John Hendy)*

PROLOGUE

In order to discover just why the ship which we now know as the *King Orry* was built, we need to return to 1926 when the French company SAGA (owned by Rothschild's Bank) founded the Alsace-Lorraine-Angleterre Societe Anonyme de Navigation.

In 1927 the name was modified to: Angleterre-Lorraine-Alsace Societe Anonyme de Navigation (abbreviated to ALA) after a partnership was forged with the London Midland & Scottish Railway Company who provided the obsolete Irish Sea ships *Rathmore* of 1908 (formerly of the Holyhead – Greenore route), *Londonderry* of 1904 (from Heysham – Belfast) and *Duke of Argyll* of 1909 (from the Fleetwood – Belfast link). After purchase they were renamed *Lorrain*, *Flamand* and *Alsacien*.

In May 1927, a new overnight service commenced between Tilbury and Dunkerque and in the following year, a fourth vessel, the *Duke of Cumberland* (a sister of the *Duke of Argyll*) was purchased and renamed *Picard*. The Thames was a much busier river then than when compared with today and there were a number of collisions and problems with fog which caused periods off service and lengthy delays in addition to a poor service. In January 1930, the Company started to use Southend Pier to land both passengers and mails in foggy weather but the service never appears to have made any money and the LMS was only too pleased to rid itself of of the loss-making route. During the summer of 1930, the *Lorrain* operated three day trips each week between Southend and Dunkerque but, inspite of carrying 6000 passengers, the revenue did little to help the ALA's ailing fortunes.

The Southern Railway took over the British side of the partnership in 1932 when the English terminal became Folkestone although the elderly *Lorrain*, with her steam reciprocating engines, was disposed-of and did not transfer with her running partners. The new route was shorter than that from Tilbury and the Southern was pleased to welcome the ALA partly to offset the loss of the Zeeland Steamship Company's Folkestone – Flushing (Vlissingen) traffic which had transferred to Harwich (Parkeston Quay) in 1926. Again the route does not appear to have made any money but the Southern Railway was, at the time, looking anxiously at the London & North Eastern Railway who had plans to run a service between its port of Harwich and Calais. Although this tidal ferry service for freight actually did operate between 1932-36, the ALA link with Dunkerque could possibly be seen as a blocking tactic. The Southern took an 80% controlling interest in ALA during 1933.

Shortly afterwards, the Southern Railway ordered three identical train ferries from the Tyneside yard of Swan Hunter & Wigham Richardson for a new link from Dover to Dunkerque. A new enclosed ferry dock was built at Dover's Western Docks although the service was delayed by geological problems – water seeping through fissures in the chalk bedrock so that it had to be lined with concrete before a service could commence. The three train ferries were named after ferry crossings on the River Thames: *Twickenham Ferry*, *Hampton Ferry* and *Shepperton Ferry*, and on 6th October 1936 the new route was inauguratated and quickly proved a great success. Apart from rail freight during the day, the service became famous for its through International passenger train – the Night Ferry which commenced operation on the night of 14th-15th October. Every evening trains of blue

Wagon-Lits sleeping cars would leave Victoria Station in London and Paris Gare du Nord for Dover and Dunkerque. There they would be shunted onto the waiting ferries which would transport passengers across the Channel while they slept, ready to arrive refreshed and ready for work in the opposite capital city early the following morning.

It was never intended that the Folkestone service should compete with the new Southern train ferries and it closed in early October, the Southern having sold the *Twickenham Ferry* to the ALA for £150,000.

During the war all three train ferry vessels became mine-layers and transports, serving for a while on the Stranraer – Larne link. The Dunkerque train ferry service was restarted in December 1947 and in July 1951, the original three vessels were joined by a fourth, the Danish-built, French-owned *Saint-Germain*.

By the late fifties there were calls for replacement vessels and British Rail's naval architects' department eventually drew up plans for three such ferries. Various Channel Tunnel projects had appeared to point to the end of the train ferry service and the original trio of ships came in for some harsh criticism from a travelling public who expected something a little more up to date. The reluctance of British Rail, their French counterparts Armement Naval SNCF and ALA (whose control had duly passed to the nationalised British Railways in 1948) to become involved in replacement tonnage at a time when a Channel Tunnel threat was hanging over them can be fully understood.

Nevertheless, things were changing and in July 1969 British Rail's new motor vessel *Vortigern* arrived at Dover from the same Swan Hunter yard that had built the original trio of train ferries.

Her design was a natural progression from the previous ships although it took over thirty general arrangement drawings to produce a vessel which was universally acceptable to the British Railways Board. The *Vortigern's* role was not to be just that of train ferry and during the summer months she was to be used to carry cars and freight on the then premier link to the continent from Dover to Boulogne. For this service she was fitted with hoistable mezzanine decks above her main vehicle/train deck and was also given a bow door and visor through which all traffic could pass onto the Boulogne linkspan. During the winter she would switch to the train ferry link, the mezzanine deck would be raised, a minor stern modification would be made to allow a proper fit

ALA's train ferry Twickenham Ferry *arriving at Dover at the end of her long career. (John Hendy)*

with the rail linkspans ashore and buffers were sited at the forward end of her four rail tracks, the bow door never being used in this role. The vessel was therefore totally multi-purpose and it seemed at the time as if most future ferries in the short sea sphere of operation would be similarly built.

The *Vortigern* was revolutionary in more than one way. Not only was she British Rail's first diesel-driven ship on the English Channel routes but she was also fitted with variable pitched propellers which, when combined with her bow-thrust unit, made her the most manoeuvrable of ships. Her arrival saw off the *Hampton Ferry* which, after operating for several months in a freight mode, was sent to Holyhead to lay-up before being sold to Greek owners. She was scrapped in Valencia, Spain, in 1973.

THE PATIENCE OF A SAINT

The order for the *Twickenham Ferry's* replacement was made on 24th November 1969, tenders having been invited from European yards. The vessel, named *Saint Eloi* in the following year (after the patron Saint of Dunkerque) was to cost in the region of 34 Fr. million (£2.93 million) and was due to be delivered on 15th December 1971.

The new ship was to be built to the west of the Italian port of Genoa some half way between the city and the French border at the yard of Cantieri Navali di Pietra Ligure. The town of Pietra Ligure is sited along a holiday coastline and was a most unlikely place for a shipyard. Although there was a certain degree of initial apprehension in some quarters concerning its choice and geographical location, the yard's tender was the most favourable and the ALA's French directors were happy that a good job would be made.

British Rail's naval architects handed-over the designs and specifications of the *Vortigern* to their ALA counterparts, lead by M. Sanner, and after having had them translated into French, then made certain modifications to the original drawings. As the new ship was to be more of a train ferry than a car ferry, it was decided to dispense with the bow door and bow visor although construction allowed a visor to be fitted at a later stage should it

The keel of the Saint Eloi *is laid at Pietra Ligure on 2nd January 1971. (Captain Emile Delohen)*

ever be deemed necessary. Neither were the *Vortigern's* hoistable mezzanine decks required for train ferry working while a larger lounge was incorporated with some cabin modifications. Basically, the new ferry was a modified sister of the *Vortigern* – their hulls were identical and the Italian yard even approached Swan Hunter for their builders' plans.

The early seventies were revolutionary in so far as ship design was concerned as design by computer was just coming into its own and it was now possible to produce drawings and detailed calculations far quicker than had previously been the case. Following experiences with their own ship, British Rail recommended to the ALA that a modification of the arrangements concerning the positioning of the watertight bulkhead sub-division in the *Saint Eloi* should be made and these suggestions were duly incorporated in the new ship's design. A further modification was the absence of a bow rudder with which all Dover ships had been fitted since Victorian times. This was used when the vessel was navigating astern as was then the practice of all cross Channel ships when approaching their berths in Dover Harbour. The *Vortigern's* Senior Master, Captain John Arthur, argued that as his ship merely swung off the entrance of the train ferry dock in Dover Harbour and did not actually navigate astern, the old-fashioned bow rudder was unnecessary and that at the slow speeds used while berthing, the bow-thrust unit alone was perfectly adequate. There were those who argued otherwise but Captain Arthur (later promoted to Commodore) was, and still is, a persuasive character and won the day.

The *Saint Eloi's* basic hull dimensions were determined by the limitations of the train ferry dock at Dover as was the positioning of the entry door into the upper garage through which up to forty cars could be driven over the port side. At Dunkerque the starboard side was used also by means of a fixed bridge which linked shore with ship. Dunkerque port was entered through one of three locks and the level of the water inside the dock system was always kept at the correct level for the successful operation of the train ferries. When arriving

By September 1971, the hull was starting to take shape.
(Captain Emile Delohen)

at very low water, the process of pumping up to rail level, particularly in the Wattier Lock, was a painfully slow proceedure. On such occasions, the train ferries were at first below the top of the lock sides and in order not to cause any damage to their bridge wings, these were sited inboard of their belting or rubbing strakes.

The slowness at Dunkerque was almost matched at Dover's train ferry dock where passengers, cars, freight and rolling stock were kept waiting on board the vessel until the correct rail height was attained. The speed aspect of the operation was one of the reasons why in 1976, the service was re-routed to the new Port Rapide at Loon Plage.

Sadly, things were far from happy at Pietra Ligure where financial problems caused delays and then strikes before the new vessel was seized by the yard's creditors. Although construction of the hull commenced on 2nd January 1971 and a projected launch date was given as the end of September, it soon became evident to all concerned with her building that the *Saint Eloi* would be very late arriving on station.

The original launch date for the train ferry *Saint Eloi* was put back to November 1971 and then rearranged for Saturday 26th February 1972 with delivery for 12th October. In the event, the ship was launched on this date by the wife of the President of the ALA, Madame Rene Margot-Noblemaire. The vessel was certainly in an advanced state of build by this time and immediately afterwards she was towed along the coast to Genoa both to be fitted-out and for her engines to be installed by other Cantieri Navali di Pietra Ligure group companies. Financial and labour problems sadly increased and saw all work cease on 1st February 1973.

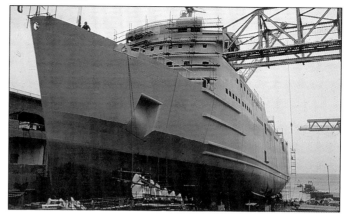

Above: Ready for launching. (Captain Emile Delohen)
Below: Madame Rene Margot-Noblemaire launches the Saint Eloi.
(Captain Emile Delohen)

The launch of the Saint Eloi *at Pietra Ligure on 26th February 1972.*

With an impasse having been reached, it was hoped that the *Saint Eloi* would be towed to another yard to be completed. Some work restarted on 1st July after the Italian Government was involved in the negotiations to free the vessel. Eventually a new company, Nuovi Cantieri Liguri, was formed to complete her although a payment of 2,775,000 lire (about £2 million) was demanded in order to do so. Normal working practices did not commence until early December 1974 and the new delivery date was now aimed at mid-December. It should perhaps be mentioned here that the ship's Chief Engineer, M. Andre Sterckeman, stood by the ship in Genoa during all this period making sure that the vessel did not deteriorate. The ALA owed a great debt to him.

The second of the original three train ferry ships to be replaced was the British Rail vessel *Shepperton Ferry* which completed service on 26th August 1972. On 12th September she was towed away for scrapping at Bilbao in Spain. The 'Shepperton' was replaced by the Norwegian-built freight/train ferry *Anderida* which took up service from Dover on 28th August with a passenger certificate for just 36.

Meanwhile, the gallant old *Twickenham Ferry* soldiered on as the first to be built of the original train ferries and the last to remain in service. The ALA had been keen to retain her and run her as a freight ship following the *Saint Eloi's* entry into service and in October 1973, she had gone off for a 15 day overhaul.

A further development of the *Vortigern* design was launched at Nantes on 12th September 1973, entering service a month late at Dunkerque on 25th February 1974. This was the SNCF Armement Naval vessel *Chartres* which because of manning problems commenced service on freight workings. As soon as SNCF switched her to passenger services (which involved more crew – stewards etc.) the vessel was immediately strikebound, blocking the linkspan in Dunkerque port between 12th – 18th March. When she returned to service, the *Twickenham Ferry* was forced to continue with the Night Ferry roster until the manning dispute was solved. Her final sailing was on 5th May after which she laid-by in Dunkerque while repairs to the linkspans on both sides of the Channel were carried out. During this period off service, she developed serious boiler problems (a constant source of concern over a period of many years) and as her passenger certificate expired at the end of the month, it was decided not to spend any more money on her and she was offered for scrap. On 26th May, the forty year old ferry left in tow for the steelworks at San Esteban de Pravia in northern Spain.

The non-appearance of the *Saint Eloi* meant that the *Vortigern* remained on the train ferry service during the summer of 1974 at a time when she should have been assisting the *Lord Warden* (3,333 gross tons, built 1952) and the *Normannia* (2.219 gross tons, built 1952) on the busy Dover – Boulogne link. At busy weekends though, the *Vortigern* was switched to car ferrying especially after the *Normannia* holed herself in Dover Harbour on 25th July and was off service for the rest of the season.

The *Transcontainer 1*, a freight ship built for SNCF Armement Naval in 1969 for their Harwich – Dunkerque container service, was now given two sets of railway tracks and ran trials into the Dover train ferry dock on 24th October. In the following month she took over the *Anderida's* roster when she went for overhaul.

The year 1975 dawned with the good news that the *Saint Eloi* was now due on 20th January. This date was certainly much closer than any of those previously given, the vessel actually arriving at Dunkerque on 1st March. After trials, the new ferry entered service on 12th March releasing the *Vortigern* on the 18.00 hrs. Dunkerque–Dover crossing. This cycle involved the 00.25 and 12.25 from Dover (the 00.25 carrying the Night Ferry sleeping cars and passengers) with the 06.30 & 18.00 returns from Dunkerque.

There had been times when the new ship never looked like arriving and during 1974, the deaths of M. Rene Margot-Noblemaire (the ALA's President between 1953-1972 and whose wife had launched the ship) and fellow director M. Henri Duval (who had been with the Company since it started and whose son Alain runs the ALA operation today) linked with the passing of the much-loved 'Twick' simply added to the misery of those who awaited the arrival of the *Saint Eloi*. She actually arrived some 39 months late. Patience of a Saint indeed!

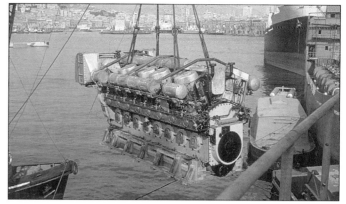

Above: One of the main Pielstick engines being lifted aboard during the summer of 1972. (Captain Emile Delohen)
Below: The long wait. Fitting-out at Genoa in October 1972. (Captain Emile Delohen)

At last! The Saint Eloi *arriving at Dunkerque on 1st March 1975 at the conclusion of her delivery voyage from Genoa. (Port Autonome de Dunkerque)*

A LOOK AROUND

Early press releases concerning the new *Saint Eloi* claimed that she would operate as a train ferry on the Dunkerque route during the winter while working as a car ferry between Dover and Boulogne for the summer season. In her latter role, she would carry 1000 passengers and 160 cars with the possibility of an additional 40 cars in her upper, side loading, garage.

Whether or not it ever was the intention to operate her in a multi-purpose mode is doubtful particularly as she was not built with a bow-door or mezzanine decks for the carriage of cars. Had the *Saint Eloi* entered service on time then it was possible that the Dunkerque route could have spared her but by the time that she entered service it certainly could not. Train ferries helping out on the car ferry routes during busy summer weekends were very common sights during the late fifties and early sixties and the 1951 built *Saint-Germain* was a popular stand-in in later years. Given adequate turn-round times, it would have been possible for the *Saint Eloi* to have loaded 40 cars across her stern and directly into her upper garage by way of the top level of the double-decked linkspan then in use at berth 4 at the Eastern Docks. Both she and the *Vortigern* had doors fitted in the after end of their upper garages to allow this but they never appear to have been used.

On 20th April the *Saint Eloi* celebrated her official 'inauguration' with a special lunch and speeches on board after a crossing to Dunkerque. It was noted that the vessel was fairly lively during her crossing from Dover and the reason behind this lay in the fact that due to the financial problems she had experienced, some components had been held-up by their suppliers and missing the odd piece in her stabiliser mechanism, her fins were then inoperable. In spite of this the occasion was a jolly affair and the Dunkerque Philatelic Club even printed a first day cover to mark the occasion.

The ship's main passenger accommodation was on decks B and C. Amenities included a boutique and a small dance floor in the main smoke room lounge forward on C deck in addition to two bars which were both on B deck – the verandah bar was aft and the other was adjacent to the galley and is now used as the crew's mess. A waiter service restaurant (below the bridge on B

Caught by the late afternoon sun, the Saint Eloi *swings at Dover, beneath the ramparts of Dover Castle, on 20th April 1975. (John Hendy)*

deck) was provided adjacent to the self-service restaurant (port side B deck) although from personal observation, the former only appears to have been used when passenger numbers demanded it. A duty-free shop and bureau de change were in constant use and on board sleeping facilities for 48 were provided in 22 standard cabins (below the train deck on deck E) and 2 staterooms (port side B deck).

On the train deck (D deck), two rails at the stern split into four on which either 35 Continental-type train ferry wagons or 10 Wagon-Lits sleeping cars plus 11 train ferry wagons could be carried. If serving as a roll on/roll off vehicle ferry, 40 x 30ft. road haulage vehicles or 160 standard-sized cars could be carried in addition to the 40 extra cars in the upper garage.

ALL CHANGE

The *Saint Eloi's* first overhaul was carried out during November 1975 at which time the *Vortigern* was called-back to work her roster. Her entry into service promised great things for the Dover – Dunkerque route which was soon to have a new French terminal, thereby speeding up turn-round times and allowing the ships to operate three instead of two round trips each day. In preparation for the anticipated extra traffic, running partner *Saint-Germain* had her passenger certificate raised from 850 to 1000 with the addition of a new lounge on top of her boat deck garage.

The new port – known as Port Rapide, Loon-Plage, Gravelines

Above: This view at the newly opened port of Dunkerque West in August 1976 illustrates the vast expanses of sand which surrounded the berths. The side loading arrangements for cars can be seen as can the lorry delivering bunkers. Below: The Saint Eloi *in the Dunkerque West train ferry berth. (John Hendy)*

or more simply Dunkerque West – opened to the Dover train ferries on the night of 4th/5th July 1976. Although the port itself had been operational for several months, the infrastructure was not then complete and without a railway station, the ferries could not make the important switch. The last sailings from the old port had been in the previous month when a strike had stranded both the *Saint Eloi* and the *Norfolk Ferry* (from Harwich) in the enclosed dock system while the 'Germain' was stuck at Dover and shuttled the trainless Night Ferry passengers across to Calais and back.

Dunkerque West was a wild and windy place and bore more resemblance to the Sahara Desert than a modern ferry port! It was completely surrounded by huge dunes and sand blew everywhere making it appear a most inhospitable place. But the fact that it was surrounded by cheap wasteland meant that there was plenty of room for expansion and that quick turn rounds could be achieved – hence Port Rapide. Having previously operated from the Quai de Douvres in Dunkerque Port, the train ferries now ran from the Quai d'Alsace and instead of taking 3 hours 45 minutes on the passage, the absence of lock gates and the ten mile difference in distance to Dover meant that the 33 mile crossing could be achieved in 2 hours 20 minutes. With this saving, six single trips could be offered every 24 hours, 15 of which were at sea. The ships were certainly more economical to operate in this manner and the increasing number of freight customers certainly liked it. Sealink put on the diminutive car ferry *Normannia* to run a freight service from Dover's Eastern Docks, the crane loaded container vessel *Rhodri Mawr* operated a daily service from Harwich (Parkeston Quay) while the SNCF vessel *Transcontainer 1* was used on the Felixstowe link – a roll on/roll off linkspan having been

During her late 1976 refit, the Saint Eloi's *blue hull paint was raised by half a deck. Here she is at Dunkerque West while her half sister, the* Vortigern, *arrives from Folkestone. (John Hendy)*

built at right angles to the train ferry berth. For the first time for many years, the Port of Dunkerque was able to compete favourably with neighbouring Calais, Ostend and Zeebrugge.

During the 'Eloi's' overhaul at the end of 1976, she received a modification in the application of her monastral blue hull paint. As will have been seen from the photographs, when she originally entered service she had been given a white strake beneath the fo'c'sle which continued through to the stern on a line midway between decks C and D. During her last years with the Company, the *Twickenham Ferry* had been similarly treated. Thus painted the new ship looked very smart, without doubt one of the most handsome vessels in cross Channel service at that time. The raising of the blue paint level by half a deck did nothing for the ship's looks but doubtless made the accountants happy.

On 23rd March 1977, ALA was wholly taken-over by British Rail although the French company continued to exist as a subsidiary of the B.R. Board. There were plans to operate the *Saint Eloi* with a British crew and place her under the Red Ensign but pressures from the French side and strikes prevented this from occuring.

In the January 1978 edition of the Sealink staff journal, Sealink News, the *Saint Eloi* appeared as number 21 in the series, 'Know your Sealink ships'. The editor, Brian Ashton, and a staff photographer had made a sailing on the Night Ferry roster and their impressions of the ship made for some interesting reading. It was reported that her shipboard facilities were second to none and that the ship carried hundreds of young people who were taking advantage of Sealink's cheap overnight fares between London and Paris. The editor then asserted that the ship's luxury accommodation was surplus to requirements for the type of passenger using the route as 95% of the 700 young people on board had their own sleeping bags. Captain Pierre Olliver (formerly Chief Officer in the passenger steamer *Cote d'Azur*) was delighted with the *Saint Eloi's* handling capabilities and considered her a fine ship from the passengers point of view. The writer considered that the ship was one of the best looking in all the Sealink fleet.

The scene, as described by the editor of Sealink News, was fairly typical at that time until, that is, much of this traffic was switched to the Newhaven – Dieppe route thus depriving Dover – Dunkerque West of extra revenue. The day-trip traffic, which had always been a feature of the previous service when passengers were taken right into the heart of Dunkerque, began to fall away. Not only were there no sailings from Dover from 09.30 until 14.50 hrs but the 19.30 return from France was the only crossing available unless the passenger wished to wait for the Night Ferry sailing at 03.30 the following morning. (Timings were later modified). Buses were available to take foot passengers into the city but some-how, the crossing had lost something of its interest and glamour and what a place to enter France through when compared to Calais or Boulogne. When Dunkerque-Ramsgate Ferries started operating in 1980 and Sally took over from them in the following year, tremendous numbers of day trippers used their services at the expense of the Dover vessels which were already beginning to feel the pinch. Quite simply it was all down to advertising.

The famous Night Ferry sleeping car service between London and Paris/Brussels closed on 31st October 1980. The rolling stock was outdated and too expensive to renew and with car ferries and easy air flight between the capitals, the need for the link no longer existed. Passengers continued to use the ships on the same timings as previously, the only difference being that their trains did not cross with them.

During the summer of 1981, Dover's last steamer, the peripatetic *Caledonian Princess* (built 1961) was called away to assist with the Channel Islands routes on which the new *Earl Granville* was off service following a serious engine room fire. At the end of June, Sealink chartered the spare Townsend Thoresen car ferry *Free Enterprise III* and on 3rd July, while alongside Dover's Admiralty Pier awaiting her 13.00 hrs departure to Boulogne, she was hit by the *Saint Eloi* which was beginning her swing prior to entering the nearby ferry dock. This minor 'brush' is mentioned here as in 1985 the Townsend ship became the Isle of Man Steam Packet's *Mona's Isle* (VI). Sadly she was to become such a problem in handling and in her inability to carry the desired loads that she was disposed-of after less than six months in service.

Eight days later, the *Saint Eloi* was placed on the Dover – Boulogne route herself, the first time that she had ever been called away on a scheduled service from the route for which she was built. This operated on a number of Saturday afternoons with the ship sailing at 13.00 hrs and returning at 17.00. The spare freighter *Anderida* covered her afternoon Dunkerque West sailing although the 'Eloi' was back in plenty of time for her trainless Night Ferry working.

In 1982 a thoughtful advertising campaign was introduced in an attempt to conjure up trade by way of enticing people to eat on board during 'Taste of France' excursions. As an extension of this, week-end cookery courses were offered in Dunkerque. Non-landing cruises for just £4.50 were advertised and the luncheon

Leaving Dover's train ferry dock in May 1975. The linkspans were lowered onto the white positioning pin on her stern thereby making the correct alignment between the rails on ship and shore. (Andrew Jones)

In February 1972, the Saint Eloi's *port propeller shaft is seen being fitted at Pietra Ligure.* (Captain Emile Delohen)

Leaving Dover's train ferry dock, this view from the rail linkspan illustrates the limitations of the ship's basic dimensions. The white building on the left is the pump house. Notice too the sloping road leading to the side loading upper garage. (Sealink archives)

and dinner menus were printed in a special brochure.

Later still, BR staff were offered special travel facilities on the route. 'Discover the railway bridge across the Channel' proclaimed a leaflet, 'did you know that an average of 110 wagons cross the Channel between Dover and Dunkerque every day'. For £6.25, a non-landing excursion (departing Dover at midday in the *Saint-Germain*) included a lunch consisting of: Mixed starters, Veal escalope in cream sauce with french fries, Cheese and Fruit tart, washed down with half a bottle of Cotes du Rhone (red),

Bordeaux (white) or Rose de Provence followed by coffee. 'From 15.20 to 17.10 hrs.' the leaflet continued,' you can watch the handling operations of wagons'. It must have been difficult to resist.

Even later still, BR staff were being offered non-landing day trips to Dunkerque West for £1.

Services were retimed as from 1st January 1982 with the *Saint Eloi* rostered to take the trainless Night Ferry passengers in both directions. Thus she sailed from Dover each evening at 23.20 hrs. and returned from Dunkerque at 04.10 with arrival back at Dover Ferry Dock at 05.30. This move, to keep hundreds of passengers away from the ancient *Saint-Germain* worked well until on 12th April, the *Saint Eloi* holed herself while berthing at Dover and had to go off service for three days for repairs. Back came the 'Germain' and back came the complaints!

On 3rd July 1982, the *Saint Eloi's* near sister, the *Vortigern* collided with the end of the pier at Folkestone and severely damaged her stern. The 'Eloi' was moved from her train ferry roster to operate the 16.10 service from Folkestone to Calais and also offered the same service on the following three days. For the next three days however, all passengers and cars were taken across to Dover Ferry Dock where they joined the ship on her home territory.

Later that summer, the *Saint Eloi* was again called out to deputise for a damaged vehicle ferry. This time it was the new French vessel *Cote d'Azur* which on 5th August had collided with her running mate *Chantilly*. The 'Eloi' crossed the harbour to Dover's Eastern Docks where she operated an afternoon round sailing to Calais before operating her scheduled overnight 23.20 train connection to Dunkerque.

More problems occurred between 16th – 19th August when

bow thrust problems forced the 'Eloi' off service while on 31st January 1983, she was blown onto a wall at Dunkerque West during a gale and again missed two days of sailings.

Summer Saturdays between 4th June and 17th September 1983, saw the *Saint Eloi* timetabled to work a round sailing from Dover Western Docks to Boulogne leaving at 16.30 hrs and returning to the Eastern Docks at 20.30 before again being in position to run the overnight passenger service to Dunkerque.

No self-respecting ferry can go through her career without encountering football supporters at some stage. The *Saint Eloi* suffered internal damage whilst on passage from Dover on the night of 29th February 1984 with England 'fans' travelling to Paris for an international match. On arrival at Dunkerque, fifteen export Rover cars were started-up on the quayside and used as stock cars. An army of French policemen marshalled the 500 sport-loving Englishmen during their return to Dover the next night.

Plans to downgrade the *Saint-Germain* to freight ferry status as from New Year's Day 1985 were met with the expected strike not only at Dunkerque but in every French Channel port to which Sealink ferries sailed. The 'Germain' was even hijacked by her crew and blocked the entrance to Dunkerque West. The dispute was settled when SNCF backed-down but the reprieve was short-lived and from 20th February 1985, the *Saint Eloi* remained as the only passenger carrying vessel on the route. Again, this state of affairs did not last long for it was announced that as from 28th September, the 'Eloi' too would be freight only. Her crew were on strike on the last day which meant that the final passengers were carried on 27th September.

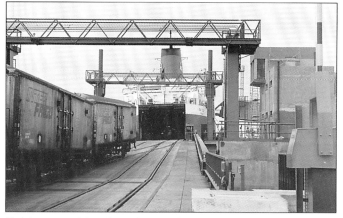

Freight wagons being shunted on board the Saint Eloi *at Dunkerque West. (John Hendy)*

The launch of the Saint Eloi *on 26th February 1972. (Captain Emile Delohen)*

Alongside at Dunkerque in March 1975, the early spring sun glistens on the Saint Eloi's *new paintwork. (Captain Emile Delohen)*

The Saint Eloi *seen half an hour out from Dunkerque West in May 1986. (Miles Cowsill)*

The Saint Eloi *was a freight-only vessel when seen here in May 1986. (John Hendy)*

UNCERTAIN FUTURE

On 17th July 1985, SNCF (French Railways) announced the order for a new super-train ferry which was to be built at the Normed yard in Dunkerque. She would be a double decked ferry – 45 pieces of 15 metre vehicle freight on her top deck and 600 metres of rail freight below – giving her a capacity four times larger than the two existing ferries. New berths would be built both at Dunkerque West where 55 Fr. million was allocated and also at Dover where some £10 million was put aside. A massive 105 metre long linkspan would obviate the need for any type of enclosed dock to accommodate the new ship and would allow an acceptable gradient for rail traffic at all stages of the 7.2 metre tidal range. The new ship was due service in 1987.

Whilst it was obvious that the veteran *Saint-Germain* had no future in the scheme of things, plans were put in hand to find further employment for the *Saint Eloi*. Following the sale of Sealink UK Ltd. to Sea Containers of Bermuda in July 1984, its naval architects (Hart, Fenton & Co. Ltd. of London) were asked to draw up plans both to lengthen her by 30 metres and also to insert an extra 5.2 metre high deck for service in the English Channel with the new train ferry. Other plans showed the ship lifted but not stretched. Several drawings were made (some as late as September 1987), and showed the ship with stability sponsons and a conversion which would accommodate 65 x 13.6 metre freight vehicles instead of the 26 then carried. The original train deck would retain its rails and could be used for rail freight or ro/ro traffic all of which would now be able to drive through the ship and out of a bow door. In such circumstances, only the forward end of her superstructure would have been retained but it was finally decided on commercial grounds that the work could not be justified and so employment was sought for her elsewhere. At one stage the *Saint Eloi* was looked at with the possibility of operating in a stretched form on the Fishguard – Rosslare route and it was believed that some £6.4 million had been ear-marked to this end.

On 16th March 1987, Dover – Dunkerque gained an extra ship in the form of the *Cambridge Ferry* (built 1963) which had been displaced from the Harwich – Zeebrugge train ferry service after it had closed at the end of the previous year. At 04.30 on 1st May, the 'Cambridge' cleared the ferry dock at Dover and headed out into the Channel in thick fog when she ran into the *Saint Eloi* which was some 700 yards off the breakwater and in the process of swinging in order to run astern into the empty dock. The British ship was badly damaged with the whole of her bow section twisted to starboard while the 'Eloi' was gashed on the starboard side of her fo'c'sle but discharged her freight at Dover before sailing for dry docking at Calais later that day. She was back on station eleven days later.

Arriving at Dover with foot passengers from Calais in July 1988, the Saint Eloi *is dressed in the livery of her charterers, SNCF Armement Naval. The fitting of the RFD escape system, in the upper entrance to the after garage, has seen the resiting of the vessel's after two lifeboats. (John Hendy)*

Damage to the starboard side of the fo'c'sle after her collision with the Cambridge Ferry *on 1st May 1987. (Andrew Jones)*

The *Saint Eloi* was briefly called to the rescue during early August 1987 when the new Dieppe – Newhaven ferry *Versailles* (a palace by name, a palace by nature – so ran her advertising) failed with engine troubles. With no ship available to take her place, the *Saint Eloi* was hastily chartered for several days until the *Vortigern* could be called from lay-up in the River Fal on 6th August.

Employment of a different nature was found for the *Saint Eloi* as from 27th March 1988 when she was called in to work a nightly freight sailing from Folkestone to Boulogne.

In the event, the new 'jumbo' train ferry *Nord Pas-de-Calais* was ready long before the new train ferry berth at berth 5 on Dover's Admiralty Pier and spent the first five months in service carrying freight between Calais and Dover Eastern Docks. The *Saint-Germain* and *Saint Eloi* therefore continued in service thanks to the hurricane force winds which had lashed southern England during

Approaching Dover during her 1988 season on charter to SNCF. (FotoFlite)

Leaving Dun Laoghaire for Holyhead in April 1989 during her unsuccessful spell on the Irish Sea. (Philip Booth)

The newly renamed Channel Entente *at Calais in May 1989 after having recently arrived from her refit at Falmouth. (John Hendy)*

CHANNEL ENTENTE
DUNKERQUE

On 23rd July 1988, the Saint Eloi *received more bow damage after a collision in Dover Harbour. She is seen here arriving at Calais that afternoon. (Miles Cowsill)*

the night of 16th – 17th October 1987, severely damaging the new train ferry installations, at the most exposed berth in the harbour, and washing most of its plant into the sea.

The final day of the old regime was on Sunday 8th May 1988, the *Saint Eloi* having previously retired for dry docking at Dunkerque on 24th April. The new service started on the 9th May while the *Saint-Germain* continued with lorry freight only for a further week after which time she was laid-up pending sale. She was scrapped in India during August.

In preparation for her new role as a passenger ship on the 'classic', seasonal, twice daily, train connected Dover Western Docks – Calais service, the *Saint Eloi* was fitted with the RFD Marine Escape System. This method of quick evacuation is simply a chute down which the public would slide into waiting liferafts in the unlikely case of an emergency. It was housed in the apertures formerly used by cars as drive on points into the ship's upper garage on C deck. The gap in the promenade immediately above this space on B deck was also filled-in allowing passengers a clear walk through to the after open deck where the RFD inflatable life-saving equipment was positioned. As for the upper garage it was converted into a large, high-capacity lounge with airline-style seats complete with a forward tea bar, and was a very similar conversion to that carried out in the *Saint Eloi's* near sisters, the *Vortigern* and *Chartres*. New toilets were also added in this area. Its conversion

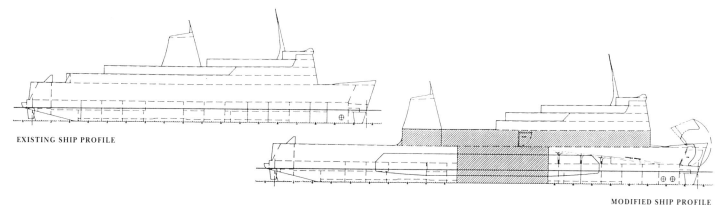

EXISTING SHIP PROFILE

MODIFIED SHIP PROFILE

Plans to stretch the Saint Eloi. *(Courtesy Hart, Fenton & Co. Ltd.)*

Leaving Dover in September 1988, the Saint Eloi's *modified bow is of special interest. (Andrew Jones)*

from garage to passenger space was not quite as simple as it might at first appear as the change of use caused a ventilation problem, it being expected that the air inside should be changed at least three times in every hour.

Another exterior alteration at this time concerned the repositioning of the ship's after two lifeboats which were resited forward of the funnel. Although from an aesthetic standpoint their removal spoiled the ship's balance, this work was essential to avoid the boats interfering with the RFD system. It also had the added advantage of providing passengers on A deck abaft the funnel with clear, uninterrupted views of the Channel.

In addition to this work, the *Saint Eloi* also received a large 'spade' fitted to her stern which allowed a good fit to the vehicle linkspans which she was to use at Dover Western Docks and in Calais. The ship also received other interior work aimed at

Leaving Heysham for Douglas in April 1990. (John Hendy)

CHANNEL ENTENTE

Mirrored in the Bidston Dock at Birkenhead in November 1990, the new King Orry is prepared for her Manx debut (John Shepherd)

The Saint Eloi *in Sealink British Ferries livery, is seen passing Lady Bay in Loch Ryan outward bound from Stranraer to Larne in March 1989. (Charles Stewart)*

Alongside at Holyhead in April 1989. (Dick Richards)

revitalising her accommodation in which Sea Containers required an undercover seat for every passenger. The most notable modifications were in the forward lounge on C deck, which received bright yellow plastic seats (a colour chosen by the French doubtless in an attempt to brighten-up the vessel's rather restrained and mainly brown interior) of a similar design to the bright red seats used in the Verandah Bar on B deck. The shop, was also converted to become a small walk-round duty-free area. The delightful oval restaurant, forward on B deck, was at first used as an overflow from the main cafeteria but latterly appears to have adopted a dual role of crew's mess and lorry drivers' lounge.

With the ambitious plans to stretch the vessel now shelved, the *Saint Eloi* was chartered to the French Sealink partners, SNCF. The service started on 27th May and continued until 24th September and for the first time the 'Eloi' appeared with an all white hull

On arrival back at Calais from her Falmouth refit in April 1989, the vessel had been renamed Channel Entente. *(Mike Louagie)*

with the word 'Sealink' written in dark blue and a red horizontal stripe either side. She looked very smart but although she now displayed something of the cruise ship image, on board all was far from well. This was not a happy period for the ship as she gained an SNCF Calais-based crew who showed a distinct lack of enthusiasm for both the ferry and her passengers. She was the subject of many complaints, the ship became rather run-down and was the cause of much embarrassment by local Sealink management who felt that the service she offered was less than what was required. After operating for a short while with her red funnel (minus the ALA logo), in mid-July the 'Eloi' received SNCF's dark red funnel colouring complete with logo – thereby reflecting her charterers.

On Saturday 23rd July, as she was leaving number 3 berth on Dover's Admiralty Pier, the *Saint Eloi* received a badly dented stem when she came into contact with the jetty at the western side of the old train ferry dock. At such a busy time in the season, she could not be spared for a long period off service and so the twisted and damaged upper stem was removed, made water tight and repainted in a matter of days. Quick, cosmetic surgery gave the damaged area back its symmetry allowing the vessel to re-enter service with the minimum of delay. For the rest of the season, the *Saint Eloi* made a very strange sight indeed with her modified bow, the lower stem still flattened but with the regulation red band painted around it to make it look as if it should indeed be there! The vessel's classification society, Bureau Veritas, gave the ship permission to continue with her temporary repairs until 30th November.

During mid September 1988, a plan was announced to transfer the *Saint Eloi* to British registry and for her to replace the *Stena Sailer* (later *St. Cybi*) on the Holyhead – Dun Laoghaire freight run. She, in turn, would operate a twice nightly service between Folkestone and Boulogne. The idea was to create extra jobs for British seamen following the closure that month of the short-lived freight service between Dover and Zeebrugge but like many other schemes at that time, it came to nothing.

At the end of the season the vessel received repairs to her damaged bow and was again laid-up in Dunkerque until, in preparation for an Irish Sea charter to Sealink British Ferries, she was in turn given its full funnel markings, the application of which always appeared rather odd as the gold 'loop' seemed to be too far aft. At this stage the red line along her hull was repainted in the standard Sealink pale blue.

The King Orry *arriving at Liverpool in April 1992. (John Hendy)*

The *Saint Eloi* was first required at the Scottish port of Stranraer between 8th January and 2nd April 1989 to stand-in during the annual overhauls of the *Galloway Princess*, *Darnia* and the *St. David* (while she was sent to Bremerhaven in Germany for refit and modification). On her return passage to Stranraer, the *St. David* had to put into the Mersey with engine problems which delayed her arrival on station. The *Saint Eloi* was therefore retained on the 2 hour 20 minute North Channel crossing to Larne and was not able to take up the second part of her Irish Sea relief season until 3rd April. This was on Sealink's central corridor route, from Holyhead to Dun Laoghaire (near Dublin), in place of the *St. Columba*. The afternoon sailing on that first day was later cancelled and the *Saint Eloi* did not commence service to Dun Laoghaire until the following afternoon at 16.50 hrs.

Sadly she was soon in trouble and the Dublin Evening Herald ran the rather dramatic banner headline, 'Mutiny on Ferry'. Blocked toilets and a generally dirty condition had caused a sit-in by some passengers in the Captain's cabin and one round sailing was cancelled while the ship was cleared up. The *St. Columba* returned to take up sailings on the route on 27th April and on the following day the *Saint Eloi* left for dry docking at Falmouth. The 1988-89 period, operating from new ports with unfamiliar crews, had been a wretched time for the ship which was certainly, through no fault of her own, earning herself a bad reputation. To quote a senior Sealink official at Holyhead, the *Saint Eloi's* stint had been "an unmitigated disaster".

Something needed to be done and when the vessel arrived back at Calais on 20th May 1989, she carried the name of *Channel*

The Channel Entente *is seen on passage between Dover and Calais during her 1989 season. (FotoFlite)*

Entente. An "entente" is a friendly understanding between states and this was an ingredient which was certainly required after the mess of the previous twelve months. Not only did it give the vessel a new image but it also allowed Sealink through their French subsidiary, the ALA, to employ a Dunkerque-based crew of their own choice with which to run the Calais – Dover Western Docks service that summer. The local unions were very much against the move but were told that the former *Saint Eloi* was sitting in a British port with a changed name ready to be sold. In order to provide seasonal jobs for French seamen in Dunkerque, the union would be foolish to refuse the offer being made to them. Common sense and some wily negotiations prevailed and the *Channel Entente* commenced service (now with a dark blue instead of a light blue line along her hull) on 26th May. It was an excellent season and brought about an end to the complaints from the travelling public.

A MANX MOVE

At this time the Isle of Man Steam Packet Company was searching for a new vehicle ferry to maintain their year-round link between Douglas and Heysham. The ferry then running the service was the chartered *Tynwald*, built on the Tyne in 1967 as the *Antrim Princess* for Sealink's Stranraer to Larne service. She had joined the Manx fleet in 1985 but in view of her age and commercial limitations, the Steam Packet wanted to find a ship which encompassed the latest safety at sea rulings and guidelines following the new regulations coming about as a result of the Zeebrugge ferry disaster. Thanks to the fact that the *Saint Eloi* had been built with the benefit of computer technology involved in the positioning of her watertight bulkheads and compartments, she both met and passed all the latest guidelines.

Above and below: Seen arriving at Douglas for the first time on 11th January 1990, the Channel Entente *passes the end of the Victoria Pier and swings in the harbour. (Captain Vernon Kinley)*

The Isle of Man Steam Packet's Tynwald, *arriving at Douglas in August 1988. (John Hendy)*

The Steam Packet had looked at a number of vessels which they thought could be suitable for their use and by the end of 1989, it appeared likely that some sort of trials for the *Channel Entente* would be carried out at Douglas and the Steam Packet's associated ports. This was essential to allow the Company's mariners and engineers to fully assess her potential and to see how her stern would fit the various linkspans.

The *Channel Entente* duly arrived at Douglas in full Sealink livery a little after 09.00 on 11th January 1990 after her passage from Dunkerque. Trials were firstly carried out at the Victoria Pier following which she berthed at the Edward Pier linkspan and during the ensuing days she sailed to Fleetwood, Heysham, Belfast and Liverpool. Whilst alongside at Liverpool's floating Landing Stage, a car was test driven into the ship's vehicle deck

Above: Trials at Liverpool. The vessel is unusually seen berthed with her port side to the Landing Stage. (John Shepherd)
Right: The Channel Entente was sold to the Steam Packet in February 1990 and retained that name during her first season. She is seen here at Douglas with the freighter Peveril. (John Hendy)

The Channel Entente *leaving Heysham on her 14.30 sailing to Douglas.*
(John Hendy)

by way of a small door which already existed in her plating. Trials were also carried out at the linkspan in the enclosed Langton Dock.

Once the trials were successfully completed, on 7th February the Steam Packet obtained approval from its stockholders to purchase the ship. The *Channel Entente* was sold at 14.30 hrs on 9th February by ALA to Vessel Holdings (Bermuda) – another Sea Containers subsidiary – and the ship was transferred from the French to the Bahamian flag. Five days later she was resold to the Isle of Man Steam Packet Company for $7 million (£4.15 million). It was decided not to rename the ship at this stage but to wait until the Steam Packet was able to stamp its own identity upon her during her first refit. Great plans were in store and it would have been a wasted opportunity of the publicity which these plans would bring to pre-empt them by localising the ship before time.

Although Sealink had recently spruced-up and modified the vessel's passenger accommodation, it is important to realise that the fifteen year old ship was rarely full during her Sealink career and that by its under use, her interior was very well preserved, if somewhat dowdy, given that she catered mainly for night passengers. It is also of interest that had the ship been retained in the English Channel, Sealink at Dover had already booked three charters for her to visit the beaches of Dunkerque during the fiftieth anniversary of their evacuation that May and June.

Still named *Channel Entente*, but now registered in Nassau (the capital of the Bahamas), with all Sealink markings painted out and wearing the historic Steam Packet funnel colours, the ship crossed from Birkenhead to Douglas on the afternoon of 17th February. On the following day (a Sunday) she was thrown open to the public on the north side of the Edward Pier. With the *Tynwald* making her final sailing for the Steam Packet that night, the *Channel Entente* set off on the first sailing for her new owners, which was delayed by some foul weather, on the following morning. During her first few weeks of Manx service, she quickly proved herself, displaying all her seagoing qualities and earning the praise of her crews and passengers alike. As for the *Tynwald*, after dry docking at Belfast she sailed to the River Fal in Cornwall to lay-up before being sold to Italian owners for further service. At the end of May she sailed for the Mediterranean as the *Lauro Express*.

Dredging No. 1 berth in Douglas Harbour to a depth of 5 metres at low water allowed the *Channel Entente* to run an uninterrupted timetable at all states of the tide.

ON BOARD THE 'CHANNEL ENTENTE'

Top left: The bridge; bottom left: The Verandah Bar with its red seats; top right: The C deck lounge contained bright yellow seating; bottom right: The car deck with railway lines still visible. (photos John Hendy)

The King Orry *in dry dock at Birkenhead following her £3.5 million refit. Notice her twin bow-thrusters. (IOMSPCo)*

MONARCH OF THE IRISH SEA

With the vessel now established, plans were made to improve her even further during her first refit. This took place at Wright & Beyer's yard at Birkenhead where the *Channel Entente* arrived on 27th September. Following a successful £2.3 million conversion and upgrading of the passenger facilities by Wright & Beyer for the *Lady of Mann* in the previous year, the contract for the modifications and improvements was given to Consultancy Services (Northern) Ltd. of Liverpool while the Steam Packet again commissioned Portland Design Ltd. of London for all the internal work. In this first phase of the ship's rebuilding, the accent was placed on comfort and convenience in all the public spaces offering different lounge areas for passengers with varying needs. The self-service cafeteria (port side forward on B deck), children's playroom (port side on C deck adjacent to passenger seating), mother and baby room (on starboard side B deck), the cruise-style Verandah Bar (port side aft on B deck) and video games room or 'Gamezone' (midship on C deck) all received attention. An executive lounge for club members with complimentary tea and coffee, newspapers and magazines and its own private toilet facilities (on the port side of B deck) was provided for those passengers who wished to sit and work en-route while for the public, telephone facilities were installed. The 200 seat video lounge (at the after end of C deck in the original upper garage), with its large screens and pop-style decor, certainly appealed to the younger traveller. Eight four berth private cabins with en suite facilities were also constructed as a block in the open area on A deck, behind the funnel. Down below the vehicle deck

The Chairman (*Mr. N.R. Corlett*)
and the Commodore (*Captain E.C. Fargher*)
request the pleasure of the company of

Mr. Mrs J.D. Duggan

at the

Recommissioning of the m.v. King Orry
by *Mrs. Jenifer Gilbey*
at *Douglas Harbour*
on *Saturday 8th December 1990*

11.30 for 12 noon
followed by
Buffet Lunch

R.S.V.P.
Mr. G. Corkish
Tel 822344

Mrs. Gilbey unveiling the recommissioning plaque at Douglas on 8th December 1990. (IOMSPCo)

(on deck E) a small lounge was specially created for lorry drivers with an adjoining couchette area offering eight sleeping spaces.

The structural alterations were designed by marine architectural consultants T.R. Little of Liverpool. On the vehicle deck (D deck), an 80 ton hydraulic powered mezzanine deck (designated M deck) capable of holding up to 60 extra cars was constructed in six individual sections from drawings prepared by the Ramsey-based Seaform Design, thereby bringing the ship's capacity up to 170. It should be added that, at some future date, this mezzanine deck could well be further extended forwards, giving the ship capacity for an extra twelve cars. When a full load of high-sided freight is on offer, the new car deck can be raised to the deck-head above. It will be remembered that in 1975 it was originally claimed that the vehicle/train deck could accommodate 160 cars but over the years the overall length of motor vehicles has risen considerably – hence the apparent discrepancy. The Steam Packet's experience showed that the main vehicle deck could accommodate only about 105 cars. A second bow-thruster was added to the original unit thereby making the ship so much more manoeuvrable at slow speeds and in gusty weather. For berthing at the Liverpool Landing Stage, a new side door and car ramp were constructed on the ship's starboard side. The whole of the ship's superstructure above the waterline, including the funnel, was shot-blasted and painted in a new high-performance coating system in addition to the go-faster stripes and Company logos.

A competition held in association with a local newspaper had invited readers to choose a new Manx name for the ship and it was not surprising that *King Orry* emerged as the clear winner. As for the meaning of this name, we have to go back to the year 1079

The King Orry *at sea showing her new Liverpool side loading door for cars, and cabin block aft of the funnel. (IOMSPCo)*

when the Norse chief Godred Crovan seized the Isle of Man and founded a dynasty which lasted for some two hundred years. His Manx name was 'King Orry'.

The choice of name was particularly happy especially as it was fifty years since the third *King Orry* so distinguished herself at the evacuation of Dunkerque before being lost by enemy action. As the *Saint Eloi*, the present ship had carried the name of that city's patron saint – a tentative link perhaps but happy one nevertheless. A Dunkerque Veterans' Service, to which representatives from the city of Dunkerque were invited, was held in the Sea Terminal in Douglas during May 1990.

As for the fifth ship to carry this famous name, some discussion ensued concerning her all-white hull with which three Steam Packet ships had been painted in the inter-war period, and also the angle of rake of the black top and rings on her funnel.

Eventually it was decided to keep the 'big white ship' image, which had proved popular, and to slightly reduce the angle of dip of the funnel markings.

With the £3.5 million refit complete, the new *King Orry* crossed the Mersey where she was on public view at Liverpool on 5th December. The following day she sailed up the Lancashire coast to Fleetwood for berthing trials before crossing to Douglas where she arrived at 19.15 in blustery conditions.

On Saturday 8th December 1990, the *King Orry* was inspected by Steam Packet shareholders before Mrs. Jenifer Gilbey (wife of Steam Packet director Walter Gilbey) officially renamed her and unveiled a commemorative plaque in the forward Compass Room on B deck – adjacent to the the restaurant. The Deputy Governor of the Isle of Man called the refurbishment, "a milestone in the history of a great company which has given marvellous service to

Evening arrival. The King Orry's *lights set Douglas Harbour aglow.*
(IOMSPCo)

the Isle of Man for over 160 years." The next day, the ship was open to the general public before taking up service with the 18.00 hrs sailing to Heysham in the middle of a fireworks spectacular.

The Isle of Man Steam Packet Company had set itself the objective of providing the highest possible quality of service with the year-round reliability of a fleet in which the Manx community could take pride. The year 1990 not only marked the anniversary of the Company's 160 years of service but also the fruition of this objective. The entry into service of the *King Orry* marked the culmination of its biggest-ever investment programme.

More dreadful winter weather (up to storm force 10) before the year was out merely reinforced the Steam Packet's view that in the *King Orry*, they were the owners of an exceptionally fine vessel indeed. Over the Christmas period, the vessel ran special sailings to Dun Laoghaire and return.

At the end of February 1991, the *King Orry* was forced off service after picking up a cable in her new bow-thrust unit. During the ensuing week out of service in dry dock, the *Lady of Mann* was hastily reactivated from her hibernation in Birkenhead Docks.

Plans for a second linkspan at Heysham were announced in the same month while at Easter, the *King Orry* also worked sailings to Belfast and Dun Laoghaire.

The second £1 million phase of upgrading the *King Orry's* passenger facilities took place during her 1991/92 refit. Consultancy Services (Northern) of Liverpool were again awarded the contract which involved the construction of a spacious new shop aft on C deck, in the forward part of the old garage, while the Summer Lounge area forward on the same deck was provided with new and refurbished seating in addition to a new coffee shop

Arriving at Dun Laoghaire on 22nd December 1991. (Gordon Hislip)

serving drinks and light refreshments. A new 'snug' bar, aptly named 'The King's Head', was installed on B deck in the space formerly occupied by the duty-free shop, and the cafeteria forward on this deck was re-equipped. Access to the lift was improved particularly for the benefit of disabled and elderly passengers. All decor was finished to the same high standards established elsewhere in the ship, interior drawings again being the work of Portland Design.

On the operational side, the *King Orry* received a new stern door, again from drawings prepared by Seaform Design, to enable her to use both the new linkspan at Heysham and also berth 4 at Donegall Quay in the River Lagan at Belfast, formerly used by P&O and Belfast Ferries. Unlike the original door, which was hinged at the top and swung upwards, the new door is hinged at its base and folds downwards to meet the linkspans. At the same time as all this was going on, a further £350,000 was being spent on modifications to the Victoria Pier linkspan in Douglas Harbour (which the vessel normally uses) while work at both Liverpool and Belfast was also taking place to greatly improve passenger facilities.

Timetable highlights in 1992 included the extension of the Douglas – Liverpool service to run every Saturday throughout the year, a regular summer Friday evening sailing from Douglas to Heysham, the extension of the Douglas – Belfast sailings through to the end of October and through sailings from Liverpool to Belfast via Douglas. The latter was a bold move as since the ending of the direct Liverpool – Belfast crossing in October 1990, there had been no main-stream passenger service linking England with Ulster. This coupled to the move to the terminal on Donegall Quay, far closer to the Belfast city centre and able to be used by the side loader *Lady of Mann* as well as the stern loading *King Orry*, also bodes well for the future. The Steam Packet will share the terminal with the revolutionary fast ferry, *SeaCat Scotland* which operates from Stranraer.

Following this further work, the *King Orry* sailed back to Douglas and re-entered service to Heysham with the 18.00 hrs sailing on Sunday 15th February. One can only speculate in what areas any future modifications will be but without doubt those thousands of passengers who sail to or from the Isle of Man cannot fail to be impressed with the totally transformed *King Orry*. Her accommodation more than equals the best on the Irish Sea and in her sea-going qualities, she undoubtedly betters them.

Long live the King!

Alongside Liverpool's world famous Landing Stage, the King Orry awaits her Saturday evening departure for Douglas. (John Hendy)

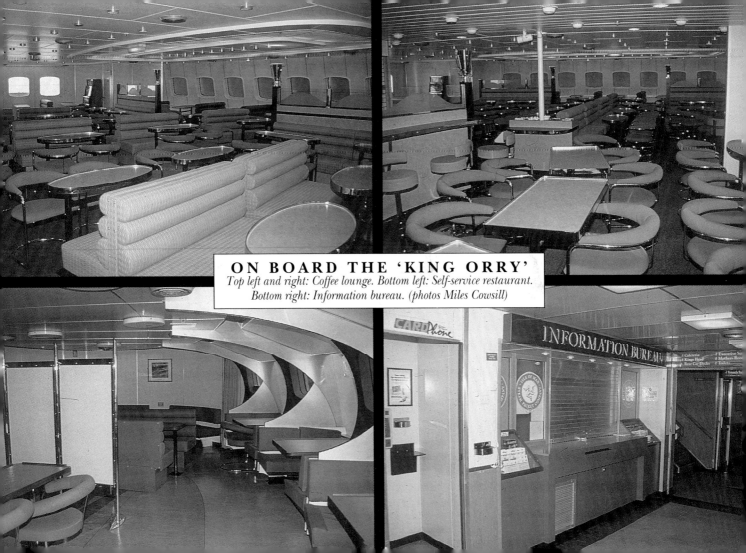

ON BOARD THE 'KING ORRY'

Top left and right: Coffee lounge. Bottom left: Self-service restaurant.
Bottom right: Information bureau. (photos Miles Cowsill)

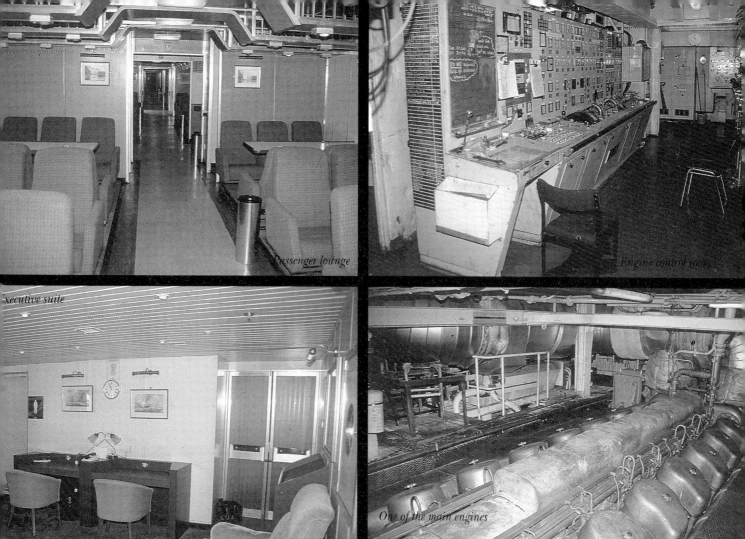

Passenger lounge

Engine control room

Executive suite

One of the main engines

The King Orry makes a splendid sight as she arrives at Heysham from Douglas. (Nick Stanbra)

KING ORRY

Previous ships of the name.

1. The Steam Packet's fourth ship and their final wooden paddle steamer was built by John Winram and Robert Napier at Douglas and was launched in February 1842. The 433 ton steamer was therefore the only vessel the Company have ever owned to have been built in the island's capital. Her engines were fitted in Glasgow and enabled her to cross between Liverpool and Douglas in something less than 7 hours. She was sold out of service in 1858 and ended her days in the eastern Mediterranean.

2. The second *King Orry* was built on the Clyde in 1871 at the yard of R. Duncan & Son of Port Glasgow. Originally some 809 tons gross, the vessel was stretched in 1888, thus lengthening her by 30 ft. and increasing her tonnage to 1104. She was broken up in the Dee estuary in North Wales in 1912 after a magnificent career of 41 years.

3. *King Orry* (III) came from the famous Cammell Laird yard at Birkenhead in 1913. Her gross tonnage was 1877, accommodation was for as many as 1600 and she carried 59 crew. Technically she was a great advance on her predecessors as she was fitted with geared turbines and she was also to serve her country well in two World Wars. Her end came violently on 29th May 1940 when during the evacuation of Dunkerque, she was bombed and sunk by enemy dive-bombers.

4. The fourth vessel to carry this illustrious name was the lead ship for a class of six similar ships built in the 1946-55 period at Cammell Laird's Birkenhead yard. Gross tonnage had risen to 2485 and she represented all that was new and good in the post war shipbuilding revival in Britain. Completing service in August 1975 she was finally broken up in the River Medway (Kent) four years later. Engines preserved at the Maritime Museum, Greenwich.

KING ORRY (V)

STATISTICS

Built .... Cantieri Navali di Pietra Ligure, Italy
Yard Number 12
Ordered .... 24th November 1969
Keel laid .... 2nd January 1971
Launched as *Saint Eloi* .... 26th February 1972
Entered service .... 12th March 1975
Length o.a. .... 114.59 metres
Breadth, extreme .... 18.62 metres
Draught, maximum .... 4.12 metres
Gross tonnage 4649
Net tonnage 1849
Deadweight 1118
Speed .... 19 knots
Renamed *Channel Entente* .... May 1989
Sold ....Vessel Holdings (Bermuda) 9th February 1990
Sold .... Isle of Man Steam Packet Company
14th February 1990
Renamed *King Orry* .... 8th December 1990
Passengers 1100
Car capacity (main deck) 110
Mezzanine deck 60
Propulsion .... 2 x Pielstick diesel engines
developing 17,200 bhp

ACKNOWLEDGEMENTS

Ferry Publications would like to express its appreciation and thanks to the following gentlemen who either assisted in the research or in the supplying of photographic material for this booklet: David Dixon (Managing Director – Isle of Man Steam Packet Company), Richard Kirkman (Passenger Manager – Isle of Man Steam Packet Company), Dennis Duggan (Public Relations Officer – Isle of Man Steam Packet Company), Tony Rogan and Donald Ripley (Directors – Hart, Fenton & Co. Ltd.), Alain Duval (General Manager – Angleterre-Lorraine-Alsace S.A. de Navigation, Dunkerque), P. Joly (Port Antonone de Dunkerque), Chris Laming (Public Relations Department – Sealink Stena Line), Paul Youden (Corporate Affairs Manager – Dover Harbour Board), Nigel Scutt (FotoFlite, New Romney, Kent), Mike Louagie, Andrew Jones, Charles Stewart, Dick Richards, Philip Booth, Gordon Hislip, Captain Vernon Kinley, John Shepherd and Captain Emile Delohen, the ship's first Master.

FERRY PUBLICATIONS

Ferry Publications was formed in 1988 by Miles Cowsill and John Hendy who had joined together to write and publish their highly successful *'Townsend Thoresen Years'*. Since then they have produced a continuous stream of titles which have covered most areas of the North Sea, English Channel and Irish Sea.

Ferry Publications launched their own quarterly journal *'British Ferry Scene'* in the Summer of 1989. Now a firmly established favourite, the magazine has quickly gained praise from both the enthusiast fraternity and the ferry industry alike.

For further information and details of current titles please write to:-

12 Millfields Close, Pentlepoir, Kilgetty, Pembrokeshire, SA68 0SA.